GREAT BRITAIN

The Poster Art of Norman Wilkinson

THE NATIONAL RAILWAY MUSEUM, YORK

NATIONAL RAILWAY MUSEUM

NRM

COLLECTION ®

Pomegranate

SAN FRANCISCO

Pomegranate Communications, Inc.
Box 808022, Petaluma CA 94975
800 227 1428; www.pomegranate.com

Pomegranate Europe Ltd.
Unit 1, Heathcote Business Centre, Hurlbutt Road
Warwick, Warwickshire CV34 6TD, UK
[+44] 0 1926 430111; sales@pomeurope.co.uk

ISBN 978-0-7649-4860-2
Pomegranate Catalog No. AA583

The National Railway Museum, York, is the largest railway museum in the world. Its permanent displays and collections illustrate over 300 years of British railway history, from the Industrial Revolution to the present day. The NRM archive also includes a fabulous collection of railway advertising posters charting the history of rail.

Pomegranate publishes books of postcards on a wide range of subjects.
Please contact the publisher for more information.

Cover designed by Patrice Morris

Printed in Korea
18 17 16 15 14 13 12 11 10 09   10 9 8 7 6 5 4 3 2 1

To facilitate detachment of the postcards from this book, fold each card along its perforation line before tearing.

The painter Norman Wilkinson (English, 1878–1971), famed for his marine canvases, produced advertisements for British railways in the time of great consolidation after World War I. Many of these posters were jointly commissioned by two of the nation's four big railway companies, less concerned about competing against each other than they were about the threat of the dreaded lorry.

After the war, army surplus vehicles flooded the market, and locally subsidized roads made shipping by automobile very attractive. The railways needed to attract the public to rail travel to compensate for this loss of business. As the engineers of the London, Midland & Scottish Railway and the London & North Eastern Railway produced faster engines and the management approved added luxuries, artists like Wilkinson recast the very experience of travel to appeal to the public.

It was to be a matter, not of porters, dining cars, and handsome steam engines, but of lyrical landscapes, sunshine, and turquoise skies. Trains were subordinated to meadows—at times the train vanished entirely. The traveler was sold not the experience of travel but the destination, whether a manor, a castle, or a mountain range.

LMS

THE NORTH WALES COAST
FROM THE GREAT ORME
by
NORMAN WILKINSON R.I.

GREAT BRITAIN: The Poster Art of Norman Wilkinson

Norman Wilkinson (English, 1878–1971)
The North Wales Coast from the Great Orme, 1923–1947
London, Midland & Scottish Railway poster
Collection of the National Railway Museum, York

707 782 9000   WWW.POMEGRANATE.COM

Pomegranate

NORMAN WILKINSON

LMS

THE MERSEY FROM RUNCORN BRIDGE

EUSTON — LIVERPOOL LINE

By NORMAN WILKINSON, R.I.

From the LMS Carriage Window Series (1)

PRINTED IN GREAT BRITAIN BY McCORQUODALE & CO. LIMITED, GLASGOW AND LONDON

GREAT BRITAIN: The Poster Art of Norman Wilkinson

Norman Wilkinson (English, 1878–1971)
The Mersey from Runcorn Bridge, 1923–1947
London, Midland & Scottish Railway poster
Collection of the National Railway Museum, York

WWW.POMEGRANATE.COM

707 782 9000

Pomegranate

THE CORONATION SCOT
ASCENDING SHAP FELL
by Norman Wilkinson, P.R.I.

LMS

The Coronation Scot, blue and silver express of the L M S Railway, runs each weekday (except Saturdays) between London and Glasgow in 6½ hours, leaving Euston Station and Central Station at 1·30 p.m. The trains consist of nine air-conditioned coaches, internally panelled in decorative woods. The locomotive Coronation Scot (No. 6220) is one of five high-speed streamlined engines designed to maintain high average speeds in all weathers over the famous West Coast Route to Scotland, which includes such difficult ascents as Shap Fell (915 ft.), and Beattock Summit (1,014 ft.). Coronation Scot attained on a test run with the train in 1937 a maximum speed of 114 miles an hour, creating a British railway record.

GREAT BRITAIN: The Poster Art of Norman Wilkinson

Norman Wilkinson (English, 1878–1971)
The Coronation Scot Ascending Shap Fell, 1937
London, Midland & Scottish Railway poster
Collection of the National Railway Museum, York

WWW.POMEGRANATE.COM

707 782 9000

Pomegranate

By NORMAN WILKINSON, R.I.

THE LAKE DISTRICT

WINDERMERE FROM BOWNESS

LMS

England's largest lake is 10½ miles long. LMS Steamers ply from Lake Side to Bowness (35 mins.) and to Waterhead Pier, Ambleside (70 mins.), calling at Storrs Pier and Lowwood Pier. The upper part of Windermere Lake has some of the finest mountain and lake colouring in the world.

The lower reach resembles a river, passing among amazingly tinted woods, rocks and hills. Near Bowness, where the lake widens considerably, there are beautiful islands. The Lake District, with its choice of yachting, mountain climbing and all sports, is one of the finest holiday districts in Britain.

PRINTED IN GREAT BRITAIN BY McCORQUODALE & CO., LIMITED, GLASGOW AND LONDON

GREAT BRITAIN: The Poster Art of Norman Wilkinson

Norman Wilkinson (English, 1878–1971)
The Lake District, Windermere from Bowness, c. 1923

London, Midland & Scottish Railway poster
Collection of the National Railway Museum, York

707 782 9000   WWW.POMEGRANATE.COM

Pomegranate

NORMAN WILKINSON, R.I.

LMS

Sweetheart Abbey owes its name to the immortal devotion of the Lady Devorgilla, heiress to the ancient Lords of Galloway, for her husband John de Baliol, founder of Baliol College, Oxford. After his death, his heart, enclosed in a silver and ebony casket, lay in a recess above the high altar in the Abbey until at her death it was buried with her. Sweetheart Abbey is near Maxwelltown, in Dumfriesshire, and originally housed the Cistercians. The principal ruins comprise portions of the church, and, some little distance away, the Abbot's Tower.

SWEETHEART ABBEY

GREAT BRITAIN: The Poster Art of Norman Wilkinson

Norman Wilkinson (English, 1878–1971)
Sweetheart Abbey, 1923–1947

London, Midland & Scottish Railway poster
Collection of the National Railway Museum, York

707 782 9000   WWW.POMEGRANATE.COM

Pomegranate

GRASMERE

By NORMAN WILKINSON R.I.

THE LAKE DISTRICT
FOR HOLIDAYS

LONDON MIDLAND AND SCOTTISH RAILWAY.

LMS Holiday Contract Tickets, 10/- Third Class, 15/- First Class, are available in this District during the Holiday Season

GREAT BRITAIN: The Poster Art of Norman Wilkinson

Norman Wilkinson (English, 1878–1971)
The Lake District for Holidays, Grasmere, 1930s

London, Midland & Scottish Railway poster
Collection of the National Railway Museum, York

707 782 9000   WWW.POMEGRANATE.COM

Pomegranate

THE SEVERN AT SHREWSBURY

BRITISH RAILWAYS

GREAT BRITAIN: The Poster Art of Norman Wilkinson

Norman Wilkinson (English, 1878–1971)
The Severn at Shrewsbury, c. 1950s

British Railways poster
Collection of the National Railway Museum, York

707 782 9000   WWW.POMEGRANATE.COM

Pomegranate

LMS

KENDAL FROM OXENHOLME

LONDON ~ LAKE DISTRICT LINE

BY NORMAN WILKINSON. R.I.

GREAT BRITAIN: The Poster Art of Norman Wilkinson

Norman Wilkinson (English, 1878–1971)
Kendal from Oxenholme, 1923–1947

London, Midland & Scottish Railway poster
Collection of the National Railway Museum, York

707 782 9000   WWW.POMEGRANATE.COM

Pomegranate

LMS   INVERNESS   LNER

by NORMAN WILKINSON R.I.

GREAT BRITAIN: The Poster Art of Norman Wilkinson

Norman Wilkinson (English, 1878–1971)
Inverness, 1923–1947

London, Midland & Scottish Railway /
London & North Eastern Railway poster
Collection of the National Railway Museum, York

707 782 9000   WWW.POMEGRANATE.COM

Pomegranate

SULGRAVE MANOR
THE GREAT DINING HALL
By Norman Wilkinson, R.I.

LMS

Sulgrave Manor, in Northamptonshire, the ancestral home of the Washington Family, was purchased by the British Peace Centenary Committee in 1914 "as a place of pilgrimage for Americans in England, and as a symbol of the kinship of the two Peoples." Originally the property of the Priory of St. Andrew, in 1539 it came into the possession of Lawrence Washington from whom George Washington was seventh in direct descent. The family lived there for over a hundred years. The original Washington Arms may be seen in the windows of the Great Dining Hall, and over the fireplace hangs a picture of George Washington by Gilbert Stuart. The Manor House is within easy reach of Northampton Station (L M S).

GREAT BRITAIN: The Poster Art of Norman Wilkinson

Norman Wilkinson (English, 1878–1971)
Sulgrave Manor, 1923–1947
London, Midland & Scottish Railway poster
Collection of the National Railway Museum, York

707 782 9000   WWW.POMEGRANATE.COM

Pomegranate

Norman Wilkinson

NORMAN WILKINSON, R.I.

LMS

Rhuddlan Castle, the scene of Edward I's Parliament in 1283, was built in the 11th Century, and though now more or less in ruins, its round towers still remain to recall its majesty in the days of its pride. Harold the Saxon captured it, and afterwards Edwin, Earl of Chester. In later days of stormy fighting the Welsh once more wrested it from William the Conqueror, but with the establishment of English rule in Wales, Rhuddlan Castle passed into the keeping of the Crown. Charles 1 restored it in the Civil War, but it was finally ravaged by the Parliamentarians in 1643.

RHUDDLAN CASTLE

PRINTED IN GREAT BRITAIN BY DAVID ALLEN & SONS Ltd, LONDON &c.

GREAT BRITAIN: The Poster Art of Norman Wilkinson

Norman Wilkinson (English, 1878–1971)
Rhuddlan Castle, 1929

London, Midland & Scottish Railway poster
Collection of the National Railway Museum, York

707 782 9000   WWW.POMEGRANATE.COM

Pomegranate

THE PASS OF ABERGLASLYN

by Norman Wilkinson

NORTH WALES

GREAT BRITAIN: The Poster Art of Norman Wilkinson

Norman Wilkinson (English, 1878–1971)
North Wales, The Pass of Aberglaslyn, 1945
London, Midland & Scottish Railway poster
Collection of the National Railway Museum, York

LMS

GALLOWAY

THE SOUTHERN HIGHLANDS OF SCOTLAND.

BY NORMAN WILKINSON.

GREAT BRITAIN: The Poster Art of Norman Wilkinson

Norman Wilkinson (English, 1878–1971)
Galloway, 1927
London, Midland & Scottish Railway poster
Collection of the National Railway Museum, York

707 782 9000   WWW.POMEGRANATE.COM

Pomegranate

LMS "ROYAL HIGHLANDER" APPROACHES ABERDEEN

BY

NORMAN WILKINSON, R.I.

GREAT BRITAIN: The Poster Art of Norman Wilkinson

Norman Wilkinson (English, 1878–1971)
"Royal Highlander" Approaches Aberdeen, 1923–1947
London, Midland & Scottish Railway poster
Collection of the National Railway Museum, York

707.782.9000   WWW.POMEGRANATE.COM

Pomegranate

TILBURY FOR THE CONTINENT

S.S. "Picard" leaving Tilbury Marine for Dunkerque

By NORMAN WILKINSON, R.I.

LMS

The nightly Tilbury-Dunkerque Service affords connections with all parts of the Continent and is the most convenient Route from the Midlands and North of England to Paris, Basle, Italy, and Central Europe.

Printed in Great Britain by JOHN WADDINGTON Ltd. LEEDS AND LONDON

GREAT BRITAIN: The Poster Art of Norman Wilkinson

Norman Wilkinson (English, 1878–1971)
Tilbury for the Continent, 1923–1947

London, Midland & Scottish Railway poster
Collection of the National Railway Museum, York

707 782 9000   WWW.POMEGRANATE.COM

Pomegranate

LMS

NORTH WALES
THE SNOWDON RANGE
NORMAN WILKINSON. R.I.

GREAT BRITAIN: The Poster Art of Norman Wilkinson

Norman Wilkinson (English, 1878–1971)
North Wales, the Snowdon Range, 1923–1947
London, Midland & Scottish Railway poster
Collection of the National Railway Museum, York

707 782 9000   WWW.POMEGRANATE.COM

Pomegranate

THE BRITANNIA TUBULAR BRIDGE
MENAI STRAITS
by Norman Wilkinson R.I.

LMS

The train which left Euston on August 1st, 1848, was called The Irish Mail, and has been so named ever since. It started at 8·45 p.m. that night, and that is its time today. But the Britannia Bridge was not yet built and passengers and mail bags had to take coach from Bangor by Telford's Suspension Bridge to Anglesey where another train awaited them.

By June, 1850 the Britannia Bridge was opened to traffic, and today Robert Stephenson's mighty engineering feat stands as a memorial to the consummate skill of the Victorian generation of engineers. Today the Irish Mail provides a day and night service to Ireland, covering the journey between Euston and Kingstown (Dun Laoghaire) in a little over 9 hours.

GREAT BRITAIN: The Poster Art of Norman Wilkinson

Norman Wilkinson (English, 1878–1971)
The Britannia Tubular Bridge, Menai Straits, 1923–1947
London, Midland & Scottish Railway poster
Collection of the National Railway Museum, York

707 782 9000   WWW.POMEGRANATE.COM

Pomegranate

NORMAN WILKINSON. R.I.

LMS

Dominated by its mighty castle, Caernarvon lies to-day in peaceful seclusion facing the quiet waters of the Menai Strait. But it has a history as stirring as that of any fortified place in our land. The first Edward built it and held it for many years against the Welsh, foremost amongst them, Owen Glendower and his hosts: and it played its part again in the Parliamentary Wars of the Seventeenth Century. The Castle is in an excellent state of preservation, and is one of the most glorious monuments to Feudalism in the Country.

CAERNARVON CASTLE

GREAT BRITAIN: The Poster Art of Norman Wilkinson

Norman Wilkinson (English, 1878–1971)
Caernarvon Castle, 1929

London, Midland & Scottish Railway poster
Collection of the National Railway Museum, York

707 782 9000   WWW.POMEGRANATE.COM

Pomegranate

LMS

ANGLESEY
AMLWCH and BULL BAY
by
NORMAN WILKINSON, R.I.

E.R.O 5335L

GREAT BRITAIN: The Poster Art of Norman Wilkinson

Norman Wilkinson (English, 1878–1971)
Anglesey, 1923–1947
London, Midland & Scottish Railway poster
Collection of the National Railway Museum, York

707 782 9000 WWW.POMEGRANATE.COM

Pomegranate

LONDON BY LMS

ST. PAUL'S CATHEDRAL

NORMAN WILKINSON, P.R.I.

LMS

GREAT BRITAIN: The Poster Art of Norman Wilkinson

Norman Wilkinson (English, 1878–1971)
London by LMS, St. Paul's Cathedral, c. 1925

London, Midland & Scottish Railway poster
Collection of the National Railway Museum, York

707 782 9000   WWW.POMEGRANATE.COM

Pomegranate

NORMAN WILKINSON, R.I.

LMS

The ruined shell of Ashby Castle brings memories of the stirring days of Mediæval pageantry, for it figures prominently in Sir Walter Scott's "Ivanhoe." At the "Lists of Ashby" were held those thrilling tournaments which that novel has made famous.

Ashby Castle was built in the 12th Century, and in the 16th for some time held Mary, Queen of Scots, an unhappy prisoner. It stood for the King in the Civil War, but was surrendered after the Battle of Naseby and demolished by the Parliamentarians.

ASHBY·DE·LA·ZOUCH

GREAT BRITAIN: The Poster Art of Norman Wilkinson

Norman Wilkinson (English, 1878–1971)
Ashby-de-la-Zouch, 1923–1947

London, Midland & Scottish Railway poster
Collection of the National Railway Museum, York

KENILWORTH CASTLE

By Norman Wilkinson, P.R.I.

LMS

One of the most famous and romantic of English Castles is Kenilworth, which should be visited by all those interested in their country's history. Many of the greatest names of the past are associated with this great stronghold, King John, Henry III, Simon de Montford, John of Gaunt, Queen Elizabeth, the Earl of Leicester and many others. It is due, however, to Sir Walter Scott's great romance of that name that Kenilworth has become a place of pilgrimage from all parts of the world, many thousands visiting it every year. To stand amongst these magnificent ruins is to live again in the glorious pageantry of the past.

GREAT BRITAIN: The Poster Art of Norman Wilkinson

Norman Wilkinson (English, 1878–1971)
Kenilworth Castle, 1929

London, Midland & Scottish Railway poster
Collection of the National Railway Museum, York

707 782 9000   WWW.POMEGRANATE.COM

Pomegranate

THE CONWAY ESTUARY
By NORMAN WILKINSON R.I.

NORTH WALES
FOR HOLIDAYS

LONDON MIDLAND AND SCOTTISH RAILWAY

L.M.S. HOLIDAY CONTRACT TICKETS, 10/- Third Class, 15/- First Class, are available in this District during the Holiday Season.

GREAT BRITAIN: The Poster Art of Norman Wilkinson

Norman Wilkinson (English, 1878–1971)
North Wales for Holidays, the Conway Estuary, 1923–1947

London, Midland & Scottish Railway poster
Collection of the National Railway Museum, York

WWW.POMEGRANATE.COM

707.782.9000

Pomegranate

BY NORMAN WILKINSON, P.R.I.

BRITAIN *in* AUTUMN

Published by THE TRAVEL ASSOCIATION, Travel Division, of THE BRITISH TOURIST AND HOLIDAY BOARD (Head Office, Queen's House, 64/65 St. James's Street, London, S.W.1, England). Printed in Great Britain by W. S. Cowell Ltd, London and Ipswich

GREAT BRITAIN: The Poster Art of Norman Wilkinson

Norman Wilkinson (English, 1878–1971)
Britain in Autumn, c. 1950s
British Tourist and Holidays Board poster
Collection of the National Railway Museum, York

WWW.POMEGRANATE.COM

707 782 9000

Pomegranate

DOVE COTTAGE GRASMERE

By **NORMAN WILKINSON, R.I.**

LMS

Dove Cottage was William Wordsworth's first home in Grasmere Vale. Here he came with his sister Dorothy in 1799; here he brought his bride in 1802; and here he wrote some of his noblest works including *The Prelude* and the famous Ode, *Intimations of Immortality*. The Cottage was formerly an Inn with the sign of The Dove and Olive Bough. It is now open to the public on payment of a small fee, and contains many pieces of furniture and other relics of England's great nature poet. In 1808 Thomas De Quincey took the tenancy from Wordsworth, and kept it for twenty years.

GREAT BRITAIN: The Poster Art of Norman Wilkinson

Norman Wilkinson (English, 1878–1971)
Dove Cottage, Grasmere, c. 1920

London, Midland & Scottish Railway poster
Collection of the National Railway Museum, York

707 782 9000   WWW.POMEGRANATE.COM

Pomegranate

PENTIRE HEAD NEAR PADSTOW BY NORMAN WILKINSON, P.R.I.

NORTH CORNWALL
BY
SOUTHERN RAILWAY

GREAT BRITAIN: The Poster Art of Norman Wilkinson

Norman Wilkinson (English, 1878–1971)
North Cornwall by Southern Railway, 1945–1949

Southern Railway poster
Collection of the National Railway Museum, York

707 782 9000   WWW.POMEGRANATE.COM

Pomegranate

LMS

WILLESDEN No. 7 BOX

MAIN LINE—EUSTON TO THE NORTH

By NORMAN WILKINSON, R.I.

From the L.M.S Carriage Window Series 282

GREAT BRITAIN: The Poster Art of Norman Wilkinson

Norman Wilkinson (English, 1878–1971)
Willesden No. 7 Box, 1923–1947

London, Midland & Scottish Railway poster
Collection of the National Railway Museum, York

707 782 9000   WWW.POMEGRANATE.COM

Pomegranate